Cyber Bullying
No More:
Parenting A High Tech Generation

by Holli Kenley, LMFT

Foreword by
Laurie Zelinger, PhD, RPT-S and Fred Zelinger, PhD:

Contents

Foreword

Bullying is an issue occurring with increasing frequency and consequence within the lives of our children, a phenomenon witnessed regularly in our role as school psychologists, private practice therapists and as parents. Significant levels of attention are now being given within schools in an effort to stem the tide, empower victims, and deflate the aggressors. Many schools have made a commitment to eradicating this pattern of reprehensible behavior and have adopted formal programs to raise awareness by actively involving students and parents in reducing, reporting and preventing bullying. Schools deal with the face-to-face issues taking place during school hours, and at times, even those incidents reported outside of school when the effects spill over into the school day. However, issues arising through venues beyond school hours are often left to families to handle by themselves. How many parents are actually prepared to recognize and address bullying when it occurs through the Internet, texting or social media avenues that our children often conceal from "prying" parental eyes? It is especially concerning because, as Kenley cites, "Many experts suggest that children do not report being violated online for fear of having their technology taken away or fear of retaliation." Likewise, Kenley teaches us that children's technological level of savvy for their age far surpasses their ability to make sound judgments regarding potential risks of on-line communication.

We know that the exploding social network brought to us by the rapidly advancing technology supporting the Internet, has altered the very fabric of human communication and interaction. Geographical distances are no longer a roadblock to immediate contact, and millions of people can be accessed simultaneously and instantly. Face-to-face discussions are being replaced by pixels on a screen and visually deciphered symbols and words in the absence of facial expression, physical demeanor, or vocal inflexion. The sender can decide to be anonymous, or if clever, easily disguise herself as someone else. Like most change, the revolution in communication brought to us by millions of linked computers and phones, carries with it both amazing benefits, and frightening pitfalls. Kenley has provided us with a powerful, accurate, and concise description of the already prevalent concern known as "cyber bullying", as well as a well thought out conceptualization of how parents can approach this expanding phenomenon.

In her "no holds barred" manual, Kenley has captured the incredible significance and power of cyber bullying, in a way that leaves the reader both shaken by its impact, and relieved by the steps offered to manage it. This pamphlet is not an expression of fear or worry; rather it is a brilliant effort to provide parents with the tools and concepts they need to both understand the potentials of internet communication, as well those needed to protect and assist their children in using technology effectively and safely. She makes her point quickly, thoroughly and accurately, leaving the reader to feel that he has the foundation to better understand, communicate and protect his child in a world with so many unknowns.

Laurie Zelinger, PhD, RPT-S and Fred Zelinger, PhD:
Licensed Psychologists

Introduction

There has been much in the news over the past several years about the dangers and abuses of online behaviors. Many of the harmful actions come from the classmates, friends, and peers of our children rather than from strangers or predators. Bullying, which has caused significant injury in the lives of countless victims throughout the years, has now become a relentless and horrifically destructive cyber force. As our children embrace a world that has been magically transformed by the wonders of technology, they also enter into an electronic culture void of human regard for one another; and tragically, they often find themselves navigating through a climate infused with revenge, retaliation and regret.

With one out of every five children having been the target of cyber bullying (Patchin & Hinduja, 2011), educators, psychologists, civil leaders and legal experts have been working tirelessly developing programs to combat it. In addition, professionals in a myriad of fields are developing strategies to intervene on behalf of the victims while searching for ways to hold the perpetrators accountable as well. However, every day, countless numbers of individuals fall prey to the abusive behaviors generated through social networking sites as well as other electronic means of communication. Sadly, as is often the case, parents/guardians who are struggling with the stressors and responsibilities of everyday life know little about the online bullying culture or aware of the importance of their role in parenting a high-tech generation.

Although there are dozens of books, videos, websites, and resources available for help in dealing with cyber bullying, the purposes of this article are to give parents/guardians a manageable number of principles and practices to incorporate into their daily lives. The parenting strategies will cover three areas of importance: Protection, Intervention, and Prevention.

Protection

Our children are growing up on a diet of technology with immediate access to worldwide social connections. Because it has become so common in our society for our children to have a cell phone, laptop, iPhone, or iPad, etc., we sometimes forget about the window of danger that is open to them. Parents would never hand over the car keys to their teens without the required number of education courses, behind-the-wheel practice hours, and supervision by an adult. And yet, we put a cell phone or a laptop in the hands of young children without adequate preparation, instruction or monitoring. We can begin protecting our high-tech children by implementing several safety measures into our parenting.

1. Know why you are giving your children access to a piece of technology or giving them permission to utilize the technology.

One excellent tool of measurement as to when a child should be given a piece of technology is for the parent/guardian to have a valid reason for doing so. These reasons might include providing for the safety of children or for emergency contacts. Caving into peer pressure or your child's rebellious attitude is never an example of responsible parenting. As children age, more access to different kinds of technology is appropriate. Again, check your adult rationale for doing so. However, with each device, parents must gradually guide their children through the various electronic mediums and venues. If your child made a new friend you'd want to know where he is going, what he is doing. The same is true with this piece of technology. Teach your children how to navigate through the new territory. If you are like many parents/guardians who are not as tech savvy as their children, have them share their web world with you while discussing and implementing safety measures.

2. Clearly explain the rules and expectations about the use of technology.

Families need to take time to talk about how to use technology responsibly. Handing it over without instruction is leading your child blindly into a dangerous environment. Whether it is a cell phone, laptop, iPad, etc., develop a set of rules and expectations about its usage:

- What is it to be used for?
- How often can it be used?
- When and where is it not to be used?
- What costs are being incurred? Who will pay?
- Who or what may be contacted? Who or what is not to be contacted?

It is mandatory that parents/guardians establish an "internet use agreement" with their children. Examples can be found and downloaded from the *Family Online Internet Safety Contract* (www.fosi.org/resources.html), *Family Internet Use Contract and Cell Phone Use Contract* (www.cyberbullying.us/cyberbullying_internet_use_contract.pdf), and *Family Contract for Online Safety* (www.safekids.com/family-contact-for-online-safety) (Patchin & Hinduja, 2011).

Although it seems like a lot of energy and time to hammer out an agreement or to put one into place, remember that we are talking about the safety of children. Like most issues in parenting, doing the hard work upfront often saves everyone from tremendous heartache in the end.

3. Monitor the use of the technology.

When parents/guardians have established some ground rules for use of technology, they then have a foundation from which to monitor the agreed-upon expectations. This serves as an excellent communication tool to revise and revisit needs as they change or evolve. Parents often think that as children get older, less supervision is needed. However, research shows that the more young people become proficient on the computer, the more likely they are to engage in cyber bullying or to be victimized. We also know that children's knowledge of technology in relationship to their respective ages far surpasses their ability to make evaluative or analytical judgments regarding the dangers and risks of online behaviors. Keeping this in mind, parents/guardians do not need to be constantly monitoring their children, but it is vital to check frequently and do so with careful examination. Other helpful hints include:

- Keeping computers, laptops, etc. within the family room, kitchen, etc. Have them visible!
- No "after hours" usage (refer to family contract).
- Talk openly about the kinds of activities, sites, etc. your children are using, discovering, avoiding, etc.

4. Implement safety measures.

In the early stages of introducing your children to healthy online communication, implement the following safety measures:

- Protect passwords. Teach children not to share their passwords.
- Protect profiles. Teach children to limit the amount and kinds of information posted online. Also, utilize the security setting provided by the online social sites.
- Obtain filtering and monitoring software.
- Monitor your child's online reputation.

5. Establish a net neighborhood.

In her book *The Bully, The Bullied, and The Bystander* (2008), Barbara Coloroso strongly suggests that parents/guardians embrace technology in the same manner as they would when introducing their children to a new neighborhood. Some of her suggestions include:

- Parents/guardians need to get to know the net neighborhood. Educate yourselves and know who and what you are dealing with. Once again, if you find yourself struggling with the cyber world, have your children teach you!

- As young children begin to venture out, supervise them and explore with them!

- As children grow and mature, give them more freedom but explain the risks as well as the responsibilities that come with that independence.

- Get to know your children's web buddies, just as you would their friends.

- Understand, parents/guardians, that your children have a "relationship" with the web. Your oversight is no less important than if it were your child's first serious boyfriend/girlfriend.

- Keep communication channels open; let your children know you are there for them, no matter what.

6. Negotiate and renegotiate the rules as age, responsibility, and needs change.

Although there are numerous theories and views on effective parenting strategies, many psychologists and clinicians agree that *authoritative* parenting commonly produces the healthiest outcomes. Authoritative parenting involves a flexible blend of following rules, of accepting responsibilities for one's behavior, and of compassionate respectful dialogue between parents and children. Structure and direction are woven into a nurturing approach. As issues surface around technology, children and parents need to deal with them openly and with meaningful accountability. Keep in mind these additional parenting strategies:

- Avoid punishing your children for the online behaviors of others.
- Avoid establishing rules and consequences that cannot be implemented.
- Avoid over-reacting to online misbehaviors. Keep the severity of the issue in mind as you administer a consequence. Remember, it is important for children to have the opportunity to correct their behaviors and to learn from their mistakes rather than to develop a rebellious spirit towards authority.

7. Parents—model healthy behaviors with technology and obey the laws in place.

Parents, we are our children's best teachers of what to do or what not to do. We must model healthy and appropriate behaviors with technology. And we must obey the laws within our respective cities, states, and countries.

Intervention

Even with safeguards in place and teaching your children to use technology in responsible meaningful ways, there are no guarantees that they will not become victims or perpetrators of cyber bullying. And, even with anti-bullying laws in 45 states, including 31 states specifying *electronic harassment,* only 6 states specifically include laws against *cyber bullying* (Patchin & Hinduja, 2011). In addition, although there are 43 states that *require school policies* (Patchin & Hinduja, 2011) addressing bullying and cyber bullying, many schools find themselves unable to implement such policies due to lack of resources, funding, or manpower to follow up on the viral number of violations. Therefore, instead of parents expending a great deal of energy blaming others for their lack of responsibility in addressing a cyber bullying attack, or relying solely on external sources to remedy the injury, parents need to be on the frontlines of intervention.

1. Have a safety plan in place.

Families must have a safety plan in place and it should be discussed with all family members. One of the most effective plans in response to being cyber bullied is the following (Hanel & Trolley, 2010):

- **Stop** what you are doing. Don't respond or react to the bullying behavior.
- **Save** the information. Do not delete. Print out a hard copy.
- **Share** the information with an adult you can trust and who can help you make a safe decision on how to handle the situation.

Many experts suggest that children fail to report being violated online for fear of having their technology taken away or fear of retaliation. In lieu of having their technology removed or grounding children from it, parents/guardians may also do the following:

- Block senders of abusive or inappropriate messages, photos, etc.
- Request that the website or social networking site remove the offensive material.
- If necessary, contact school personnel or legal authorities.
- Change passwords when violated.
- Take down profiles or remove self from online site or venue.

2. Let your children know that it is safe and necessary that they come to you (or another trusted adult) if they are cyber bullied.

It is extremely important that children do not feel alone when victimized. Research has suggested that children are reluctant to disclose being cyber bullied because nothing is done to help them even after it has been reported to an adult. Take time to talk with them about how they are feeling; help them to implement the appropriate safety measures (discussed in #2); and continue to monitor their online reputations. Parents/guardians—above all—be available and be supportive.

3. Understand the difference between web buddies and real friends.

Children today have countless numbers of online acquaintances. It often becomes difficult for them to differentiate between web buddies and real friends. With peers changing their friendship status as easily as changing a pair of shoes and with online bullying being so prevalent, it is quite confusing for children to understand what a *real friend is*. As parents, it is our duty to teach them about the characteristics of true friendship and of the importance of how we treat one another.

Helping them to understand that real friends do not betray one another (through bullying or other means) will help children in clarifying their confusion and in moving through their hurt.

Tragically, research has also suggested that many children who do not see a difference between the real world and the cyber world find it completely natural to treat others inhumanely (Li, 2010). The thinking is that if the damaging behavior online can be acted out with limited consequences, it is permissible to do so in person. Thus, it is all the more important for parents/guardians to spend time with their children talking about the harmful effects of online and offline bullying and of the real person at the receiving end of such attacks.

4. Take advantage of counseling or support groups.

In the past several years, many young people have taken their own lives because of relentless, abusive acts of cyber bullying. It is extremely important for a child who is experiencing ongoing victimization to seek out support from a school counselor, professional therapist, or an age-appropriate support group. Victims tend to withdraw, become depressed, and feel completely lost and isolated. Parents/ guardians, do not hide behind the belief that the bullying will go away or will just get better over time. It will not.

In addition to person-to-person support, there are a couple of excellent online websites available to help and support young people who have questions about bullying or who are being targeted (Patchin & Hinduja, 2011). These sites are interactive, where children can connect with others who have experienced similar experiences:

- *Cyberbullying 411:* www.cyberbyllying.com
- *Cyber Mentors:* http://cybermentors.org.uk

5. Be aware of retaliation and of the relationship between victims and bullies.

In their research, Kowalski, Limber, and Agatston (2008) have shown that there is a strong relationship between traditional bullies, cyber bullies, cyber bully victims, and victims. For example, if a child is exhibiting traditional bullying behaviors, it is likely that he is also bullying others online, and he may even be a victim of cyber bullying. We also know that cyber victims frequently cross over to cyber bullying behaviors. And yet, there are times when individuals are "pure victims" or "pure bullies" with no other roles being played out. This is important information for parents/ guardians as they investigate their child's involvement in bullying behaviors and seek out effective interventions.

Regardless of a child's relationship with cyber bullying, it is never a healthy option to seek revenge or to continue the retaliation. Teaching our children how to protect and take care of themselves as well as how to treat others respectfully not only serves them, but it is a critical step toward curtailing the rampant cyber virus.

6. Continue to talk with your children, monitor activities, and negotiate or amend rules as needed.

Parents/guardians, stay involved with your children and in their relationship with technology. Don't assume that everything is alright—*know that it is*. Revisit your "family contract or agreement" from time to time. Make changes or additions as circumstances, age, and needs dictate. Use the topic of technology as a vehicle to stay connected to your children, to communicate with them, and to demonstrate how much you care about their worlds—real and cyber.

Prevention

Even after our children have completed their driver's training, taken their driving exams, and have shown the maturity and responsibility to drive a car, these preparatory safety measures will not prevent them from being involved in an accident. This is a painful realization, but it is true. Although it is not always possible or even realistic, we, as parents/guardians, must acknowledge that the only way to absolutely prevent our children from being injured by some-one or something is to never allow them access to that person or thing. It is absurd to entertain the idea of excluding tech-nology from our society; however, we can have an honest discussion about the destructive behaviors nurtured by electronic communication, and we can learn how those behaviors are reinforced by the workings of technology. By educating ourselves about the *causal factors* of a cyber bulling culture, we can open our minds to healthier ways of interacting and relearning social ways of being. So, we can begin to eradicate the breeding grounds of this contagious pathogen and prevent its spread.

1. Educate yourself and your children about the relationship between technology and the individual and its impact on us as social beings.

Parents/guardians, this is extremely important. When our children communicate through any source of electronic means, they participate in an *indirect relationship*. In other words, they are not *face to face* with someone else. This dynamic of being separated from the presence of another human being creates feelings of detachment. As these feelings of detachment and disconnect take hold, two additional forces come into play: anonymity and power differential. With these two forces in play, a child is at liberty to say whatever he wants, to as many people as he likes, with no feedback as to how damaging or injurious the words may be to the victim.

Over time and with repeated usage of electronic means of communication, our children's psychological makeup is indeed impacted. Studies in Singapore suggest that "technology reduces the sensitivity an individual has toward others and his/her environment." (Ang & Goh, 2010). Also, other important developmental changes include the following:

- Children experience a disconnect with the *real* world and with *real* relationships (Hinduja & Patchin, 2009).

- Children's behaviors become increasingly disinhibited (Dooley, Pyzalski, & Cross, 2009). Due to a lack of oversight, children feel more freedom to express themselves in inappropriate ways.

- Children experience a loss of empathy for others or lack of human regard for one another (Ang & Goh, 2010).

- Children begin to exhibit feelings of contempt: a sense of entitlement, intolerance toward differences, and a liberty to exclude others (Colorosso, 2008).

- Children demonstrate a decline in positive social/personal interaction or in the development of healthy social skills (Ang & Goh, 2010).

Although these characteristics may seem unimportant or insignificant in the overall development of a child, with continued online usage without the balance of interpersonal communication, these ways of thinking show themselves as antisocial and narcissistic personas called *cyber bullies*. And, as these unhealthy personalities permeate the cyber world, they fuel and feed the online bullying culture.

2. Educate yourself and your children about how technology itself reinforces unhealthy behaviors.

As children experience the feelings of autonomy, of power, and of detachment in their cyber world, and as they develop unhealthy behaviors and characteristics, parents and their children are largely unaware of how the technology itself conditions and reinforces those behaviors. In other words, technology sustains and motivates the bullying persona in the following ways (Hinduja & Patchin, 2009):

- There is no immediate feedback loop or consequence to deter the bully from the behavior. Moreover, there is little or no accountability for wrongdoing.

- The bully does not have face-to-face contact with the victim. Therefore, he is removed from the impact on the victim which typically acts as a deterrent to aggressive behaviors.

- The bullying act gains infamy by remaining online for lengthy periods of time with countless users weighing in. This serves to empower the bully.

- The bully is protected through anonymity, pseudonymity, and fake profiles. Again, there is no consequence or accountability for the behavior.

- Because of the ease of responding, technology erases the "reflection time" typically used to think through or to evaluate an action. This is replaced with habitual impulsivity.

- Although more research is needed, there is a suggestion that the bully's behavior is reinforced by the "sense of anticipation/excitement he experiences between the sending of the attack and the time when the victim actually is made aware of the attack." (Dooley, Pyzalski, & Cross, 2009).

- Although the role of bystanders varies, many bullies are motivated/empowered by offline and online participants (Li, 2010).

Parents/guardians, we must acknowledge that although there are countless valuable uses of technology, there are also risks to our children and to their psychological well-being. Being aware of those consequences will help as we move forward in a more balanced approach in our relationships with and without technology.

3. Adopt a family philosophy of 'cyber balance'.

It is critical that families adopt a lifestyle that is not entirely built around technology. As is true of the foods we put into our bodies, what we feed our minds will affect our levels of emotional wellbeing and connectedness. Parents/guardians must adopt a family philosophy of balancing their use of technology with other family routines (Trolley & Hanel, 2010).

- Begin with a family assessment. By asking some tough questions, take an honest inventory of your family's use of technology.
  - ➤ Is there healthy balance of use of technology in your home?
  - ➤ How much time are family members spending on the use of various devices?
  - ➤ How much time are you spending together as a family or as individuals without the use of technology?
  - ➤ Do the quantity and quality of technological use interfere with being present and available for one another?

- Set up family guidelines to implement *cyber balance*.
  - ➤ Designate periods of time during the day where no technology is allowed. Suggestions include meal time, car or travel time, and/or in the evenings when homework and chores are done.
  - ➤ Designate "zones" and "times" that are "tech free". Honor those commitments!
  - ➤ Take time during the weekend to have a "tech-free" day. Have a family day of doing chores,

> planning fun activities that do not include technology, and/or just spending time together.
> ➢ As a family, frequently revisit topics of accepting responsibility and accountability for one's actions in the cyber world and the real world.
> ➢ As a family, brainstorm other ways to implement *cyber balance*.

4. Find ways in your family to experience direct interaction, to empathize with one another, and to serve others.

To combat the online norms of indirect interaction, of detachment from one another, and of self-serving behaviors, parents/guardians must plan and implement healthy social behaviors (Trolley & Hanel, 2010). The following activities will help to promote direct interaction, to nurture empathy for one another, and to create opportunities to serve others.

- During the designated "tech-free" periods, take time to be present and available for one another. Talk together face to face, without interrupting. Really listen to each other. Give each member of the family time to share ideas, thoughts and feelings.
- Replace "tech games" with real-life activities, sports, hobbies, or games. Enjoy the person/s who are with you "in the present". Let them know how important they are.
- Each day or each week (at the minimum), do something good for someone in your family without being asked. Then, do something special for a friend, a peer, or someone you know who needs a helping hand. Look for ways to do good—be an example to others.
- With your church, synagogue, mosque, temple, youth group, sports club, or favorite organization, seek out ways to help others who are less fortunate.

- Speak up or stand up for others who are being criticized, bullied, made fun of, or humiliated in any way. Don't stand and watch in silence; be a friend when a friend is needed.

- Seek out ways to be present and available for others.

5. Parents/Guardians, model the behaviors that you expect from your children.

Parents/guardians, we have tremendous influence in our children's lives, at least early on, or until we prove ourselves to be unworthy of it. Model the balanced behaviors that you expect from your children. In return, they are more likely to respect you, and thus, are more willing to follow your lead.

Conclusion

Technology is here to stay, as it should be. Children will continue to embrace its magnificence while navigating through safe as well as dangerous territories. As parents and guardians, it is our duty to teach them how to protect themselves from injury, and it is our responsibility to intervene when they need our support and help. Most importantly, in order to prevent them from experiencing the destructive antisocial side-effects from an over-indulgence of technology, we must guide, monitor, and balance their intake. This high-tech generation needs our best parenting; they deserve no less.

Face to Face: Unwired

It was last summer, but I remember as if it were yesterday,
The image forever etched upon my soul.
A family gathered together sharing barbeque with close friends,
No technology to fill the space—only conversation and eager ears.

With plates of lean steak, bowls of salads, and baskets of breads passed among us,
The young adults home from college filled their bellies and we ours.
Dad bantered with his grown children and laughter sprinkled over the table,
No technology to distract attention—focus on the speaker and minds present.

The flow of food and drink continued for hours and yet it flew by,
Family stories told from years past and we too told our own.
Mom's nurturing spirit brought warmth to more delicate conversation,
No technology to interrupt the flow of empathy—each person available for the other.

Stomachs beckoned for a pause, but soon desserts galore arrived,
And a calm settled in as the sun started to disappear.
Plans, dreams, and hopes were explored—each one creating a sparkle,
No technology to dim the glow—similar visions captured and shared by all.

Darkness came too quickly as final words embraced the night,
With winks and spars, young adults took their cues to clear and to clean.
Older adults were left to say their thanks, goodbyes, and next-times,
No technology still—only eyes on eyes and arms reaching for hugs.

Walking to our car, I felt full for the first time in a long time,
Realizing that what I devoured was so rare, so missed, so needed.
No social pathogens—just hungry hearts feasting on a buffet of human connection,
And savoring each and every morsel of being—of simply being present for one another.

Bibliography

Ang, R. P., & Goh, D. H. (August 01, 2010). Cyberbullying among adolescents: The role of affective and cognitive empathy, and gender. *Child Psychiatry and Human Development*, 41, 4, 387-397.

Coloroso, B. (2004). *The bully, the bullied and the bystander*. New York: HarperCollins.

Dooley, J., Pyzalski, J. & Cross, D. (2009). Cyberbullying Versus Face-to-Face Bullying: A theoretical and conceptual review. *Zeitschrift fur psychologie/journal of psychology*, 217 (4), 182-188.

Hinduja, S., & Patchin, J. W. (2009). *Bullying beyond the schoolyard: Preventing and responding to cyberbullying*. Thousand Oaks, Calif: Corwin Press.

Patchin, J., & Hinduja, S. (2011). *Cyberbullying prevention and response: expert perspectives*. New York, NY: Routledge.

Li, Q. (January 01, 2010). Cyberbullying in High Schools: A Study of Students' Behaviors and Beliefs about This New Phenomenon. *Journal of Aggression in Maltreatment and Trauma*, 19, (4), 372-292.

Trolley, B., & Hanel, C. (2010). *Cyber kids, cyber bullying, cyber balance*. Thousand Oaks, Calif: Corwin Press.

About the Author

Holli Kenley is a licensed Marriage and Family Therapist in the state of California. She holds a Masters Degree in Psychology with an emphasis in Marriage, Family, and Child Counseling. She first became interested in promoting the wellness of others in the early 1990s by volunteering time to lead support groups for women struggling with Premenstrual Dysphoric Disorder (PMDD). This experience was the motivation behind her first book, *The PMS Puzzle*, as well as the impetus to return to graduate school to become a licensed therapist.

Holli has worked in a variety of settings: a women's shelter and transitional housing, a counseling center, and in private practice. Counseling with adolescents, teens, young and older adults, Holli's areas of special training and interest include sexual trauma and abuse, betrayal, addiction, codependency and cyber bullying. Holli is the author of numerous published articles and in 2010, she authored her second book, *Breaking Through Betrayal: And Recovering the Peace Within*. Recently released is her first e-single, *Betrayal-Proof Your Relationship: What Couples Need To Know And Do*.

In addition to her work as a therapist and an author, Holli enjoys speaking at workshops and conferences. For the past two years, Holli has been a peer presenter at the California Association of Marriage and Family Therapists' Annual Conferences. In 2011, Holli spoke on "Cyber Bullying: The H1N1 of Technology—An Analysis of Causation & Implications for Intervention." Holli will be a peer presenter at CAMFT's 48th Annual Conference in May 2012 speaking on "Triaging Cyber Bullying: Protection, Intervention & Prevention."

Try these other empowering titles from Holli Kenley, M.A.

Learn more at www.HolliKenley.com